Ingeborg Santor / Ruth Ingram
Selected Poems

Selected Poems
Ausgewählte Gedichte
by Ingeborg Santor

Translated by Ruth Ingram

Bibliographische Information der Deutschen National-
bibliothek: Die Deutsche Nationalbibliothek verzeichnet
diese Publikation in der Deutschen Nationalbibliographie;
detaillierte bibliographische Daten sind im Internet über
www.dnb.de abrufbar.

Herstellung und Verlag: BoD – Books on Demand,
Norderstedt

ISBN 9783744819084

Ingeborg Santor (born 1941 in Koblenz) was employed as editor in various publishing houses; after that she worked freelance as editor and text-writer for museums until 2003.

Several of her poems and short stories first appeared in journals and newspapers. Some essays, documentary features and poems were broadcast on Nordwestdeutscher Rundfunk and Südwestfunk. Her first book publications were two collections of poems: 'Amsellied und Krähenschrei' and 'Im Schneelicht' plus a selection of short stories. Some poems and prose texts were translated into Polish and printed in literary journals and anthologies in Poland.

Ingeborg Santor has also translated some English poetry, including poems by John Rety. Together with him and Ruth Ingram she has had the collection 'Between Languages' published by Hearing Eye. In particular she worked on Judy Gahagan's long poetic biography of King Ludwig II. of Bavaria: 'Tours around the Soul of Ludwig' appeared bilingually in 2009.

In 2014 her collection of poems 'Lichtfänger' was published and in 2016 a storytelling book about her childhood 'Frühe Zimmer, kleine Jahre'.

Ruth Ingram (born 1927 in Berlin) was formerly a principal lecturer and course Director of a postgraduate course in Applied Social Studies. Later she worked with textiles and photography. She exhibited in various galleries in London and in her own home. She now mainly concentrates on translating German poetry. She also organises a poetry translation workshop which meets quarterly. Participants call themselves 'Camden Mews Translators' and have published two anthologies of translations from French and German entitled 'Over the Water' and 'Across Frontiers'

She has had two collections of translations published: 'Selected Poems by Hans Sahl' and 'Selected Poems by Arno Holz' as well as the anthology 'In Exile. Poems by Hilde Domin, Mascha Kaléko and Hans Sahl'. Several of her own poems and some translations appeared in six publications of the Highgate Poets magazine.

A long poem by Hilde Domin was published in 'Modern Poetry in Translation' and two of her translations of poems by Hans Sahl were printed recently in the poetry journal 'Fenland Reed'.

This book is dedicated to my friend Ruth Ingram who has translated most of my poems since 1999. I'm much obliged to Ruth for her sensitive work, her encouragement and patience.

Ingeborg Santor, June 2017

Calendar Leaves

Vorhut
oder: Von der Prophetie der Eichen

Neben dem Winterjasmin
füllen Krokusse ihre
Kelche mit frühlingswarmem
Sonnengelb, kleine Vögel
machen sich wichtig, als wär
ihr Reviergesang schon eingeübt
und selbst die alten
erfahrenen Apfelbäume schicken
eine Vorhut Knospen
raus ins verfrühte Leuchten.

Nur die Eichen, kahl
am Waldrand, ringen
die Äste, als müssten sie
den entgangenen Winter
beschwören. Oder als
wüssten sie, was kommt.

Vanguard
or the oaks' prophecy

Next to the winter jasmine
crocus fill their chalice
with spring-warm yellow
little birds make themselves
important, as if their territorial
song was much practised
and even the old experienced
apple trees send their
advanced buds out
into the too-early light.

Only the oaks, bare
at the edge of the wood
wring their branches
as if they had to cast a spell
on the missing winter. Or as if
they knew what was to come.

Hasenjahr

Weit offen das Augenpaar in
der heimlichen Sasse, kalt
überm Feld noch
von Osten der Wind, doch schon
klopft dies hasenfüßige Herz
gegen sein Winterfell, wittert das
sprießende Frühgrün, riecht
fetten Sommerkohl, hört
herbstliches Geläut
jagender Meuten.

The year of the hare

Eyes wide open
in the secret hide
the wind in the field still
cold from the east, but
already his timid heart
beats against the winter coat
senses the sprouting early green
smells fat summer cabbage
hears autumn tumult
of a hunting pack.

Treibhauskinder

in die Vase gestellt:
erste Tulpen, eine blaue
Hyazinthe, Birkenzweige,
eine verschlossene Rose –
jeden Abend trag ich sie
ins Dunkle, Kühle. Damit
sie langsamer sterben.

Hothouse children

placed in a vase:
first tulips, a blue
hyacinth, birch twigs,
an unopened rose –
every evening I carry them
into the dark, the cool
so that they die more slowly.

Verirrt

Unterm Märzblau nichts als
Gleißen: Schnee, so weit
mein Blick den Weg spurt.

Auf einmal
im Weißen: Feuerfunken! Ein
Schmetterling – sonnetrunken

hebt er sich, schwebt
kahlen Ästen zu, dem blauen,
dem eisklaren Himmel.

Gone astray

Under a March blue, nothing
but glistening, snow as far
as my eye follows the way.

Suddenly
in the white: fire sparks!
A butterfly – sun-drunk

it lifts itself, hovers towards
bare branches and the
blue ice-clear sky.

Präsentation

Als *Eyecatcher*
hell im Frühlicht:
Auslegeware in dreierlei
Grün, samtweicher eins
als das andre! Kontrast-
stark dazwischen gesetzt
ein sattes Braun – sehr
raffiniert komponiert und
großzügig hingebreitet
hügelan die Felder, drüber
ausgespannt dieses Blau...

Sage noch einer,
April verstünde nichts
von *Merchandising!*

Display

To catch the eye
bright in the early light
carpets laid out in three
different greens, each more
velvet-soft than the other.
Between them in stark contrast
a rich brown – very
ingeniously composed
the fields, generously
spread upwards over the hills
and spanned over by this blue...

If someone still says
April knows nothing
of display!

Die Schöne

Jeden Morgen läuft sie
in großer Eile an meinem
Küchenfenster vorbei – nie ohne
einen raschen Seitenblick
rüber zu mir. Sichernd?
Ich ziehe die freundlichere
Deutung vor, nicke
ihr zu, aber da ist sie schon
vorüber, immer von rechts
nach links eilt sie jeden
Morgen über das begrünte
Garagendach.

Natürlich hat sie den
gelbesten Schnabel, die
schwärzesten Federn, die
flinksten Füßchen – wie
wird sie erst fliegen!

The Beauty

Every morning she runs
in great haste past my
kitchen window – never without
a quick glance over to me –
to be sure? I prefer
the friendlier meaning, nod
to her, but then
she is already past. Always
from right to left
she hurries every morning
over the green-growing
garage roof.

Naturally, she has
the most yellow beak
the blackest feathers
the swiftest little feet –
how then shall she fly?

Frühjahrslaune

Lerne gerade, das Wasser
zu kauen, den Wind zu trinken,
breche ab vom Brot der Bäume,
schlürfe Erdgeruch, Grasgeruch,
frühestes Licht – in der Kehle
ein blankes Gelächter.

Spring mood

Just learning to chew the water
to drink the wind,
break bread from the trees
slurp the smell of earth, of grass
the first light – in my throat
a bright laughter.

Eingekocht

Der Duft der Sommeräpfel
wie sie köcheln im Zuckersud
ganz leicht zerfallen zu Mus
hellgelb wie die früheste Sonne –
und ich sehe sie immer noch
liegen und leuchten im feuchten
Morgengras wie in kleinen
Nestern aus Licht.

Cooked apples

The scent of summer apples
as they simmer in sugar syrup
fall lightly apart to mush
bright yellow like early sun –
and I still see them
lying and glowing in damp
morning grass, like in little
nests of light.

Sommers Zenit

Tag für Tag
unterm züngelnden Haar
der Medusenblick.
Ausgebrannt
der blaue Scherben
versteinerte Weißglut
nicht Himmel mehr, nur
grelle Last.

Die kurze Nacht lang
im Geheimen
sing ich Regenmacherlieder.

Summer's Zenith

Day after day
under flickering hair
Medusa's gaze.
Burned out
the blue, fired
in white heat
no longer sky, only
a glaring burden.

The short night long
secretly I sing
rainmaker's songs.

Glühen wie kurz

Kaum dass der Sommer
den Lupinen hohe Kerzen
in die grünen Hände gibt
mit Farben wie sonst keine
und ich sehe sie glühen wie
kurz vorm Verlöschen – schon
legt sich Herbst auf die Haut.

Brief glow

Hardly has the summer
given the lupins tall candles
into their green hands
with colours like no others
and I see them glowing as if
to be extinguished shortly – than
autumn lies its hands on me.

Herbstgänge wieder

– und immer das Schauen.
Unstillbar der Hunger

nach diesem durchsichtig
leuchtenden Himmel, dem keine
Farbbezeichnung nahe kommt

nach dem wildbraunen Fell der
Äcker, dem Gelb daneben, das
sich noch hält an schwarzem Geäst

nach dem sterblich-unsterblichen
Rot der Ilexblätter am Weg
zwischen verlassenen Schrebergärten.

Herbstgänge wieder –
das Schauen

Autumnal walks again

– and always looking in
unrequited hunger

for this transparent
glowing sky, that no
artist colour approaches

for the wild brown coat of
the ploughed fields, next the yellow
that is still hanging on black branches

for the mortal-immortal red
of the illex leaves on the wayside
between abandoned allotments.

Autumn walks again –
that looking

Herbst

Ich wohne außerhalb. Die Stadt
rauscht in den Ohren, fällt nicht
ins Auge. Was mein Fenster rahmt
kunstlos nenne ich's Glück: Wald,
Wiese, Himmel, ein Tal voller Jahreszeit –
Herbst. Und wie Herbstblätter fielen
die Stare heut aus dem Wind, schwarz
flackernde Zeichen. Ich lese sie auf.

Autumn

I live out of town. It can't be seen
but murmurs in my ears.
What my window frames, artlessly
I call it happiness: wood, meadow,
sky, a valley filled with season –
autumn. And like autumn leaves
to-day the starlings fell out of the wind.
I read the black flickering signs.

Beim Öffnen der Hände

Blätter aufgelesen,
denen die Herbstfarben
abhanden kamen.

Beim Schließen der Hände
ein harsches Geräusch –
was übrig blieb, fällt

beim Öffnen der Hände.
Verwitterte Wünsche
fallen mit.

At the opening of my Hands

I gathered the leaves
that have lost their
autumnal colours.

At the closing of my hands
a harsh sound –
what remained falls

at the opening of my hands.
Withered wishes
fall too.

Novembertee

Wie das grüngolden
ins Sieb fließt über die dunklen
Blätter der Minze, Kindheitswiese
im kräuselnden Dampf: Gräser
und Mohn, Margeriten und blaue
Glocken im Wind – nur
die Minze nirgends, Lippen-
blütler, zart lila... Ich sauge den
Blätterduft, sommerheiß werd ich
die Wiese trinken, Minze und
wieder gefundene Zeit.

November Tea

How it flows green-gold
into the sieve over the dark
leaves of the mint – childhood
meadow in curling steam: grasses
and poppies, marguerites and blue
harebells in the wind – only
nowhere the mint with its
delicate lilac bloom... I breathe
the leaf-scent, I will drink
the summer-hot meadow, the mint
and re-discovered time.

Reste

Ein paar Ähren stehen da
im Wind, bleich längst und
steif wie Greise nicken sie
mir zu. Aber weithin sichtbar
das Rot der Beeren,
Hagebutten und rote
Lackreste auf altem Holz.

Remains

A few wheat stalks stand
in the wind, long since pale
and stiff like old men they nod
to me. But a long way visible
the red of the berries,
rose-hips and red
lacquer on old wood.

Winter-Haiku

Gehäkeltes Eis
an meinen Fensterscheiben.
Wintergardinen.

*

Gefiedertes Eis
an meinen Fensterscheiben.
Kein Vogel zu sehn.

Winter Haiku

Knitted ice
at my window panes.
Winter curtains.

*

Feathered ice
at my window panes.
No bird visible.

Stille Post

Beuge mich über
den Brief, den schwarzes Geäst
mir in den Schnee schreibt, lese
Rätselworte, schwer
zu sagen, welcher Sprache.

Chinese whispers

Bending over
the letter, which black branches
write for me into the snow, I read
puzzle words, difficult
to say, in which language.

Vorrat

Ein Frühlingshimmel
sorgsam eingelagert – den
spanne ich aus, wenn's
allzu finster wird und
kalt.

Provision

A spring sky
carefully kept in store – that
I will open out if it becomes
altogether too dark and
cold.

Catching Light

Morgenbesuch

Sitzt da und guckt
mir ins Fenster mit
blanken Augen, pickt was
Unsichtbares da und da
von meiner Fensterbank.

Äugt mich an, geht auf
und ab, zeigt das Gefieder
– sehr hell, darüber schmal
ein augenschwarzes
Ringelband.

Zwischen uns nur
Glas. Und dass ich
keine Flügel habe.

Morning Visit

It sits there and looks
into my window with shiny
eyes, pecks at something
invisible, here and there
from my window sill.

Eyes me, walks up and
down, shows it's bright
plumage with a narrow
ink-black band
round his neck.

Between us only glass
and that I haven't
got wings.

**Beim Gehen
auf den Flutsaum zu**

Welle auf Welle
Grünland, Sandland
und graublau das
Meer flutet Welle auf
Welle dem Sand zu
dem Grün zu
Wasserlicht, Sandlicht
Grünlicht wogt
auf mich zu und gleitet
wieder ins Weite – davon

**While walking
towards the tide line**

Wave on wave
green land, sand land
and grey-blue the sea
flows wave on wave
towards the sand
towards the green
water light, sand light
green light flows
towards me and glides
away again – into distance.

Kalligraphie
oder: Von der Geduld des Windes

Schön schreibt der Wind
in den Sand am Meer.

Stetig, jahrhundert-
tausende lang, schrieb er
und schreibt der Geliebte
der See seiner unsteten
Freundin unzählbare
Zeilen, ferne dem Flutsaum
und fern ihren nassen
Lippen schreibt er

dies eine Wort Welle
immer
die eine Wort Welle

zarteste Zeilen – und kein
Wellenwort je, keines
dem anderen gleich.

Calligraphy
or: The Wind's patience

The wind writes beautifully
in the sand by the sea.

Constantly, a hundred thousand
years, the lover of the sea
wrote and is still writing
to his inconstant friend
innumerable lines,
away from her wet lips
he writes

this one word wave
always
this one word wave

most delicate lines –
and no wave-word ever
like any other

Mauersegler

Über dem planen
Land schwarz blitzende
Schnitte ins Blau, helle
Schreie aus Hunger und
Lust, sirrende Pfeile
des Sommers – wie sie
den Himmel ritzen mit
spitzen Stimmen
den Tag lang und immer
noch abends überm
erhitzten Land.

Swifts

Over the open plain
black lightning cuts
in the blue, high calls
of hunger and joy
vibrant arrows of summer –
how they etch the sky
with pointed voices
all day long and on
still into the evening
over the heated land.

Lichtfänger

Gehe hier jeden Tag
meiner Profession nach, die Augen
geübte Kescher für jeden Glanz:
das Blitzen des Gräserhaars
der Dünen, die Helle stiebenden
Sandes, ein Blinken im Watt,
am Flutsaum das Schillern
der Wanderinselchen aus Schaum.

Und manchmal so seltene
Beute, wie sie der langsam
schwingende Flug der Schwäne
mir zuwirft aus blendendem
Gefieder – als hätten sie Licht
viel zu viel. Über mir halte ich
sie in der Schwebe für immer.

Catching Light

Walking here every day
I follow my vocation, my eyes
practised nets for every lustre:
the glitter of grass-hair on the dunes,
the brightness of scattering sand,
a gleam in the mudflats, and
on the tidal edge the shimmer
of little wandering islands of foam.

And sometimes, rare catch,
a slow-winging flight of swans
send me a dazzling white
out of there plumage – as if
they had far too much light.
I hold them suspended
above me for all time.

Gewitterbericht

Aufgeführt
hat sich das!
Den Linden unter
die Röcke gepfiffen
straßauf, straßab gejohlt
krakeelt, den Häusern
eins aufs Dach
gekracht, Schlag
auf Schlag hell:
eine Weißglut
vom Himmel
und schon überall
Wasser, ein
klatschender Fall
ein rauschender
Schwall, ein –

Wässerchen.
Tröpfelt noch
trippelt noch
trielt... War da
was?

Thunderstorm

What a performance!
Whistled under the skirts
of the lime trees
yelled up the street
and down the street
howled, crashed
on the house roofs
blow on blow
brilliant white fire
from heaven: and now
everywhere water
a splashing fall
a rushing swell, a –

rivulet.
A dripping still
a dribble still
a trickle – was that
something?

Nördliche Fahrt ins Graue

Wie das wabert zwischen Warft und
erbleichendem Land, stammlos
gespenstern entfernte Bäume,
weggelöscht ein Krähenstrich,
sterbensrot Astern in
fliehenden Gärten. Nur
das Marschgrün standhaft
den Schafen zulieb, meinen
hungrigen Augen. Wann, wie bald
ein Unterwasserland, versunken.

Northerly Journey into Grey

How it sways between wharf and
the land turning pale, ghostly
distant trees without trunk
a streak of crows wiped away
red-dying asters in
fleeing gardens. Only
the marsh green constant
for the sheep and for my
hungry eyes. When, how soon
to sink? A land under water.

Spökenkieker-Lied

Um den Haubarg schleichen
wieder die Geister, ein bleiches
Gelichter, aus Feuchte geboren
das bläht sich und dreht sich, das
windet sich, schwankt, im Nichtlicht die
Bäume, die Mauern versinken, schon
schwindet das Dach. Ein Wehn ohne
Wind treibt das Schwindelgesindel
abendlang, nachtlang ums wankende
Haus. Und es warnt dich kein Laut.

Spooky Song

Round the old farmhouse
the ghosts are prowling again
a pale rabble born in the damp
they swell and turn, they squirm
and sway, in the unlit the trees
the walls sink, already the roof
is vanishing. A blowing without wind
drives the scoundrels all evening,
all night round the swaying house –
and no sound warns you.

Donaukiesel

Aus dem steinigen
Gemurmel am Ufer
dieser eine

der schmiegt sich mir
in die Hand, als hätt' er
da hingewollt

mit seiner weichen
Kühle, der hell
gerahmten Mitte –

Fenster, durch das
der Fluss immer weiter
weg fließt.

Danube pebble

Out of the stony murmur
at the river bank
this one

is pliant
in my hand, as if it
wanted to be there

with its soft
coolness, the framed
bright centre –

window, through which
the river constantly
flows further away.

Donau stromauf

Wir reihten die Tage auf Silberschnüre
die über dem Wasser glänzten im Wind
wir zogen stromauf in dem grünen
Gewoge, tag-nachtlang der rauschende
Wechselgesang.

Und unter den Füßen vibrierten die Kessel
ihr Stampfen quoll auf in den Ohren, ging
unter im Schaben der Wellen am
Schiffsrumpf, ein Suchgeräusch: wo

endet das Harte, lässt Fließendes ein?
Jede Nacht, bei gedrosselter Fahrt
schwappte der Strom uns in unruhige
Träume, in schwankenden Schlaf.

Donau stream-up

We had thread the days on silver cords
that shone over the water in the wind
we sailed up-stream on green waves
day-nightlong the rushing song-change.

And under our feet the engines vibrated
their pounding rose up in our ears,
went down in the scraping of waves
on the hull, a searching noise

to where the ship might end and
let flowing come in. Every night
with a slowing down, the stream washed
in our restless dreams, swaying sleep.

Die Krutynia
(Masuren)

Fließen wie dunkle Haare im Licht
Fließen wie Stundenglassand immer fort
fließen ein lautloses Hingleiten über
Bäume und Himmel und Wolken die
grüne Spiegelwelt schwankend
im ständigen Ungefähr hell
über Dunkel und dunkel im Hellen
die Hand fasst ins Kühle das rinnt
durch die Finger so glänzend ins
Fließen ein Windhauch spurt Linien
ritzt flüchtige Zeichen ein Ton tropft
im Röhricht da träumt der gefangene
Kahn seine Kette sich silbern zer-
fließend im Fluss – Fluss sage ich
sage dies Wort: Fluss

The Krutynia *
(Masuria)

Flowing like dark hair in light
flowing like hourglass sand, ever
flowing, a soundless gliding
over trees and sky and clouds
a green mirror world swaying
in constant uncertainty, light over
dark and dark in the light
cool water runs gleaming through
fingers, returns to the flowing
a breeze traces lines, inscribes
fleeting signs, a tone drips
in reeds where the tied boat
dreams that its chains dissolve silver
in the river – this river ever flowing
in the flow of my voice

* River in Poland

Sein Geheimnis

Wie er untertreibt mit diesem kleinen
Silberglanz im Perlenohrring
dem Fünkchen aus einer Drehbewegung
der Pinselspitze, scheinbar absichtslos
damit nur umso mehr die sanften
Mädchenaugen schimmern, die
eine Frage wissen, eine Antwort
vielleicht fürchten und doch: wünschen

und wie zart er den Schmelz auf
die eben sich öffnenden Lippen
getupft hat über dem weißen
Kragen, der all das warme Licht
herunter zu kühlen vorgibt – nur
um den scheu erwartungsvollen
Blick über die Schulter noch tiefer
leuchten zu lassen.

His Secret *

How he underplays this little
silver shine in the pearl earring
the spark made with a turn
of the pointed brush, seemingly
without intention, so that the girl's
soft eyes shimmer even more
knowing a question and perhaps
fearing an answer still desired.

And how delicately he dabs
the glaze on the just opening
lips over the white collar
that seems to cool down
all the warm light – only
to let the shy expectant
gaze over the shoulder
glow still more deeply.

Jan Vermeer: 'The girl with the pearl earring'

Le bel excentrique
Eric Satie

Sind das Regentropfen, die falln
in die Seine? Oder zögernde
Schritte, das Klicken
seines Spazierstocks durch
Montmartre? Dann aber: Tanz,
Fingerwirbel, sein Lachen hüpft
flusswärts die klingende
Treppe hinab, Steinchen lässt er
übers Blanke flitzen, flipp –
doch dann gravitätisch
mit großer Geste die Stufen
wieder hinauf, der Stock klopft
Befehle – und fliegt davon.
Freihändig schlendert Monsieur
über die Tasten, pfeift sich eins,
lacht. Über mich und meine
dummen, zu langsamen Ohren.
Die horchen ihm lange noch nach.

Le bel excentrique
Eric Satie

Are those raindrops falling
in the Seine? Or hesitant
steps, the click
of his walking stick through
Monmartre? But then: dance,
whirling fingers, his laugh
jumps down the ringing steps
towards the river. He flips
little stones over the blank
surface, flip – but then
gravely with great gestures
the steps up again, the stick
beats commands – and flies off.
Monsieur free-wheels leisurely
over the keys, whistles and
laughs at me and my
ignorant, too slow ears
that listen still, long afterwards.

Winterlicht

Im Novemberlicht
auf dem Weg ein kleiner Stein.
Wie groß sein Schatten!

*

Hell überzuckert
das karge Land. Aus der Nacht
gefallenes Licht.

*

Ins Eis gebannte
Kreise aus Schatten und Licht.
Batik des Winters.

Winter Light

In November light
on the way a little stone.
How great its shadow!

*

The barren land
brightly sugared. Light fallen
out of the night.

*

Bound in ice
circles of shadow and light.
Winter Batik.

Ohnegleichen

Wenn ich Wörter hätte für das lange
Schwinden des Lichts am Abend
leiseste Wörter, fast wie nicht
gesprochen, aber angefüllt mit dem
Schimmern des vergehenden, fast
vergangenen Tages, Flüsterwörter
gehaucht wie das Schon-nicht-mehr-
Türkis am schon nicht mehr hellen
noch lange nicht dunklen
Streifen Himmel vor der Nacht,
Abendwörter ohnegleichen – ich hätte
keine Worte.

Without Equal

If I had words for the long
fading of evening light,
soft, quiet words, almost
as if not spoken, but filled
with the shimmer of dying,
nearly departed day
whispered words on the breath
like the touch of vanishing turquoise
on the strip of sky before nightfall
no longer light, still not yet dark,
evening words without equal –
there are no words.

Später Gast

Zum Abend sage ich:
Komm rein. Hier kannst du
unbehelligt
rüber dunkeln in die Nacht.
Ich nehme an, auch du
hast genug gesehn
für heute.

Late guest

I say to the evening:
Come in. Here you can
darken over into night
undisturbed.
I take it, you too
have seen enough
for to-day.

Alter Freund

Nachts auf dem Heimweg
von Laterne zu Laterne, wie da
zwischen dieser und der nächsten
Helligkeit mein Schatten mir
aus den Schuhen wächst, schwarz
und schnell mich überholt, groß
wird, ein Riese, der sachte ent-
schwindet vorm nahenden
Lichtschein – und wieder
sich anschleicht.

Old Friend

At night on my way home
from lantern to lantern, how
between this and the next
illumination my shadow
grows out of my shoes, black
and quickly overtakes me
becomes large, a giant, who softly
disappears from the approaching
light – and creeps
back again.

Perpetuum mobile

Wache nur
schlaf
oder träume und schreib
in den Sand –
am Ende wirst du
brechen, leis
wie die Welle
am Kiesel:
ein Wispern
im vergeblichen
Gesang des Meeres.

Perpetuum mobile

Only wake
sleep
or dream and write
in the sand –
at the end you will
break softly
like a wave
on a pebble:
a whisper in vain
lost in the song
of the sea.

Years gone by

Kinderzimmer

Sauber und anständig
aufgeräumt alles und
weg gepackt – so ist es
ordentlich, sagte der Vater.

Das Kind
fand sich lange
nicht wieder.

Children's room

Clean and decently
tidied, everything
put away – so it is
correct, said the father.

For a long time
the child did not
find itself again.

Wieder gefunden

Mein Brunnenland:
so klar im Wind
der kleinen Stimme Ton
so frisch im Schnee
der kleinen Füße Spur.

Darunter muss
ein Weg sein. Und
ein warmes Haus ist da
wo ich noch immer
wohne.

Found again

My land of springs:
the small tone of a voice
so clear in the wind
the tracks of little feet
so fresh in the snow.

Down there must
be a way and
a warm house
where I still
live.

„Mondnacht"

Das Haus im Wald
vierzehn war ich, saß
mit angezogenen Knien auf
der Fensterbank, himmelte
den Mond an, stundenlang
– über schwarzen Bäumen
ein Wunder an Sanftheit
und samtenem Licht.

Wie bösartig grell jetzt
wie bissig hell er die Nacht
durchsticht, Strahlenfinger
in meinen Schlaf stößt
in erschrockene Augen –
vorm Fenster sein hartes
kleines, ein gnadenloses
Gesicht.

Moon night *

The house in the wood
I was fourteen, sat
with drawn up knees
on the window sill, adored
the moon, hours long –
over the black trees
a miracle of gentleness
and velvet light.

How evil the glare now
how biting the light
to pierce the night
finger beams stab
into my sleep,
in startled eyes –
before the window a hard
small merciless face.

* *The German title refers to a famous*
poem by Joseph von Eichendorff

Verlustanzeige

Eben kam mir
– Folge eines Blickes –
meine Seele abhanden.
Flog davon
mit der Schnelligkeit
eines Wimpernschlages
mitten hinein
in das blitzende, gleißende
Schwalbengewitter
hoch oben dort im
wolken-, atem-, grenzenlosen
Blau.

Was fang ich
jetzt an hier unten
ohne die
glücklich entflohene
Schwalbenschwester?

Reporting a loss

Just now
as your glance fell on me
I lost my soul.
Flew away with the
beat of an eyelash
into the midst
of a glittering, glistening
swallow-storm
high up there
in the cloudless
breathless, unbounded
Blue.

What shall I do
now down below
without the
happily escaped
swallow sister?

Für eine Amsel

Singender Vogel im Baum
hingetuscht gegen
den Abendhimmel:
Als wär dein Lied
zu groß, so bebt
deine Kehle, schutzlos
Schönheit verströmend
singst du
bis in die Federspitzen.
Inbrünstig singst du
singst
als sängest du
um dein Leben.

For a blackbird

Singing bird in the tree
colour-washed against
the evening sky:
As if your song
was too great
so your throat
trembles defenceless.
Streaming beauty
you sing fervently
sing to the tips of
your feathers.
Sing as if
for your life.

Vorweggenommener Abschied

Ich schweig in deinen Schlaf
du atmest in mein Wachen.
Der Blick, der mich nicht traf
das nicht geteilte Lachen –
sie wachsen an.

Von Mund zu Mund ein Land
der nicht gesagten Worte
und dein und meine Hand
sehr weit entfernte Orte.

Ich trau dem Traum nicht mehr
und hör nicht auf zu träumen.
Du schläfst und atmest schwer.
Wir werden uns versäumen.

Anticipated parting

I'm silent in your sleep
you breathe into my waking.
The look that did not meet
the laughter that wasn't shared –
all have increased.

From mouth to mouth a land
of words which were not said
and now your hands and mine
in very distant places.

I trust the dream no more
and yet don't cease to dream.
You sleep with heavy breath.
We'll never meet again.

Zuletzt

Es ist alles gesagt.
Deine stummen Hunde
hetzten längst
mein letztes Wort
zu Tode.

Pfeif sie zurück.
Vom versteinten Gefühl
ist kein Hausfriedensbruch
mehr zu fürchten.

Atme auf.
Schließ die Tür.
Lösch das Licht.

Es ist alles gesagt.

At last

Everything has been said.
Your mute dogs
have long hounded
my last word
to death.

Whistle them back.
There is no need to fear
trespass from my feelings.

Breathe easy.
Shut the door.
Put out the light.

Everything has been said.

Sonntagsfrühstück solo

Rücke also die leeren
Stühle zurecht, entzünde
die Kerze – beidhändig
gieße ich Milch und Kaffee
in den Becher, während
der Nachrichtensprecher
mir schon die Welt reicht
in unverdaulichen Brocken.

Die Speise also bereit
und das Messer
dem Tag zu begegnen.
Ich kaue die Flocken
das Bittre, das Süße
der Trauben, das Brot.
Im Radio leis Albinoni.

Sunday breakfast solo

Put the empty chairs
straight, light the candle
pour the milk and coffee
with both my hands
into the beaker
while the news reporter
hands me the world
in indigestible lumps.

The food thus
prepared and the knife
to meet the day.
I chew the flakes
the bitter, the sweet
of grapes, the bread.
On the radio: Albinoni.

Auf einmal

mitten im Trubel der
Fußgängerzone – fast wär ich
vor Schreck (und so gerne)
dir gleich in die Arme gefallen
wie unter die Räuber – hast du
was gesagt? Und was ich?
Nichts mehr weiß ich, aber
genau, dass deine Augen
noch immer so blau wie eh
und je mich ansah'n und
dass dein Haar langsam weiß
wird, wie meins, und dass
du, wie damals, meine Hand
länger als nötig gehalten
hast. Und dass wir da
standen, nah –

Suddenly

in the midst of the throng
on the pedestrian path
– in shock (and so gladly)
I nearly fell into your arms
as if swept off my feet – did you
say something? And did I?
I don't know anymore, but
only that your eyes
still as blue as always
looked at me, and that
your hair like mine
is turning white, and
that you held my hand
like at that time
longer than necessary.
And that we stood, close –

Meine Jahre

Meine Stunden
meine Tage
meine Jahre gehn
und aus all den
flüchtig aufgeschlagenen
Seiten sehn
unverwandt
die großen Fragen.
Und ich bange:
Wen
werd ich rufen
wenn mein Inneres
plötzlich schwiege?

My years

My hours
my days
my years go past
and out of all the
hastily opened pages
the great questions
steadily look at me.
And I am frightened:
Who
shall I call
if my inner being
would suddenly
fall silent?

Verlässlich

Ich hab meine Trauer
hochglanzversiegelt
mit meinem hellsten
Gelächter.
Verlässlich
unterm schönen Schein
der Oberfläche
trägt sie mich so
wenn all meine glänzenden
Stricke reißen.

Dependable

With my brightest
laughter, in high gloss
I have sealed my grief.
Dependable
under the beautiful
surface shine
it carries me
when all my glossy
threads break.

Astern

Grau im Frühlicht.
Nur das bange
Rot der Astern
färbt den Morgen.

Ach Astern-Rot
verwundbarste
der Farben –
Abschied, Trost
und Sommers letzte
leise Klage.

Grüß die Astern.
Denn es kommen
blumenlose Tage.

Asters

Grey in early light.
Only the anxious
red of the asters
colours the morning.

Oh aster-red
most vulnerable
of colours –
parting, consolation
and summer's last
soft complaint.

Greet the asters.
Flowerless days
are coming.

Luftbuchung

Meine Wörter wollten
nicht bei mir bleiben

schon gar nicht wollten
sie auf Papier.

Da hab ich sie
in den Wind geschrieben.

Wind publication

My words didn't want
to stay with me

most of all they didn't want
to go on paper.

So I wrote them
into the wind.

Ablagerung

Tiefer graben
unter die weichen
Schichten gesunkener Jahre.
Da, im Sediment
steinalt ein Schmerz –
gerundet, aber
nicht zu heben.

Deposit

Digging deeper
under the soft
layers of sunken years.
There, in the sediment
an ancient pain –
rounded, but
not possible to lift.

Erinnerung
(Montenegro)

Hoher Himmel
ferne Horizonte
über dir ein Blau, das schweigt.
Weit das leere, übersonnte
Land, aus dem die Stille steigt.

Fels und Ginster
steingewordene Wege.
Hinter dir zerfällt das Haus.
Brich dein Schweigen,
komm und lege
Netze der Erinnerung aus.

Memory
(Montenegro)

So high the sky
horizon far away
above you a silent blue.
Wide the empty sun-filled
land where stillness rises.

Rock and broom-bush
paths turned to stone.
A house behind you in decay.
Break your silence,
come and lay out
the nets of memory.

Im Kopf meiner Mutter

Im Kopf meiner Mutter
ist Feuerpause, ein feindlicher
Friede. Sie holt aus der Asche
was sie nur findet: verstümmelte
Wörter, zerbrochene Sätze, sie
sammelt die guten, die schlechten
ins Töpfchen, das ist ihr
zerschossen zum Sieb.

*

Das Wort, das meine Mutter
sagen will, zerfällt ihr im Mund. Sie
weint ihm nach und mich trifft aus
den alten Augen ein Kinderblick.

*

Gestern
sprangen ihr die Wörter
auf die Zunge wie gerufen.
Heute
sind sie unauffindbar wie
Nadeln im: du-weißt-doch
wo

*

Meine Mutter will mir
dringend was sagen:
Ich muss doch noch
sagt sie. Ihre Hand
sucht auf dem Tisch:
Dings! sagt sie, *na
sag schon!*

Ich rede und rede und
finde kein Wort.

*

Ich rede mit meiner Mutter, als ob
nichts wäre. Als wäre alles, wie
es war.

Und höre mich reden, höre
meine Sätze mir weglaufen, ihren
verirrten Wörtern nach.

*

Wie gesagt
sagt meine Mutter
und hat
nichts gesagt.

In my mother's head

In my mother's head
is a cease-fire, a hostile peace.
She takes out of the ashes
what she can find: mutilated words
broken sentences, she collects
the good and the bad in a pot
which has been shot through
like a sieve.

*

The word my mother wants to say
crumbles in her mouth. She
weeps for it and I get
a child's look from the old eyes.

*

Yesterday
words sprang from
her tongue as if called.
To-day
they are impossible to find
like needles in: you-know-where
don't you?

*

My mother wants urgently
to say something to me:
I have to still
she says. Her hand
searches the table
Thinggy, she says, *well
say it then!*

I talk and talk and
find no word.

*

I talk with my mother, as if
nothing was the matter, as if
everything was as it always was

And hear myself talk, hear
my sentences run away from me
after her lost words.

*

As I said
says my mother
and has
said nothing.

75

Antwort

Warum fragt meine
Mutter fragt mich fragt
jeden der an ihr Bett
kommt: *Warum
kann ich denn nicht
schneller sterben?*

Ich höre sie immer
noch fragen, als sie
lange schon und
schnell gestorben ist.

Answer

Why, does my mother
ask, asks me asks
everyone who goes
to her bedside: *Why
can't I die
more quickly?*

I still hear her ask
long since she died
and quite quickly.

Winter

So klar dieser Himmel
dass Eisglanz die Wimpern
mir zackt, den Blick schärft
ins schattenlos
knirschende Licht.

Da hisse ich Segel
den Wegen entgegen:
lautlos vorm Mund
weiße Schrift.

Winter

So clear the sky
that ice gloss barbs
my eyelash
sharpens my sight
in shadowless
biting light.

Then I set sail
on my way: soundless
before my mouth
a white script.

Wachtraum

… und wär ein Felsstein
blass und kalt
und wäre grünbemoost
und schwer und alt
und wär das Feste
mitten im Verschwimmen
wär das Verstummte
jenseits aller Stimmen
und wäre lange
Salamanders Sonnenort
und wär das Schweigen
hinter allerletztem Wort.

Und wär das Lauschende
in eine andere Welt
das mundlos sanft
im Irgendwann
zu Staub zerfällt.

Day dreaming

… I were a rock
were pale and cold
green with moss
and heavy and old
constant in all
uncertainty –
the voiceless one
beyond all voices
and were for long
a lizard's sunny place
and were the silence
after the final word.

And were the listener
to another world, who must
softly and soundless
sometime
fall to dust.

Inhalt / Contents

*Most of the poems chosen for this selection were taken from
'Lichtfänger', published by Books on Demand in 2014.
Thirteen poems have been published in the earlier collections
'Amsellied und Krähenschrei' and 'Im Schneelicht' (out of
print).*

Index of English Titles